Tsunamis

WITNESS TO DISASTER

In the world there is nothing more submissive and weak than water. Yet for attacking that which is hard and strong, nothing can surpass it.

—Lao Tzu,
Chinese Philosopher

Tsunamis

WITNESS TO DISASTER

JUDY & DENNIS FRADIN

NATIONAL GEOGRAPHIC

WASHINGTON, D.C.

Founded in 1888, the National Geographic Society is one of the largest nonprofit scientific and educational organizations in the world. It reaches more than 285 million people worldwide each month through its official journal, NATIONAL GEOGRAPHIC, and its four other magazines; the National Geographic Channel; television documentaries; radio programs; films; books; videos and DVDs; maps; and interactive media. National Geographic has funded more than 8,000 scientific research projects and supports an education program combating geographic illiteracy.

For more information, please call 1-800-NGS-LINE (647-5463) or write to the following address:
National Geographic Society
1145 17th Street N.W.
Washington, D.C. 20036-4688
U.S.A.

Visit us online at www.nationalgeographic.com/books

For information about special discounts for bulk purchases, please contact National Geographic Books Special Sales: ngspecsales@ngs.org

For rights or permissions inquiries, please contact National Geographic Books Subsidiary Rights: ngbookrights@ngs.org

Library of Congress Cataloging-in-Publication Data available available on request.

Hardcover ISBN: 978-0-7922-5380-8
Library Edition ISBN: 978-0-7922-5381-5

Printed in the United States

Series design by Daniel Banks, Project Design Company

The body text is set in Meridien
The display text is set in ITC Franklin Gothic

Photo Credits
Cover, John Russell/ AFP/ Getty Images; Back, Bettmann/ Corbis; spine, N. Silcock/ Shutterstock; 2-3, Rick Doyle/ Corbis; 5, Hermann M. Fritz, Georgia Institute of Technology; 6, Jose C. Borrero, University of Southern California; 8 both, IKONOS satellite imagery by GeoEye/ CRISP-Singapore; 9, AFP/ Getty Images; 10 both, Joanne Davis/ Polaris; 11 left & right, Joanne Davis/ Polaris; 11 bottom, Mark Pearson; 12, PH3 Tyler J. Clements, United States Navy; 13, Louis Evans, Curtin University of Technology; 14, Image: S. Lombeyda, Caltech Center for Advanced Computing Research; V. Hjorleifsdottir and J. Tromp, Caltech Seismological Laboratory; R. Aster, Reprinted with permission from *Science* Volume 308, Number 5725 (20 May 2005); 15, U.S. Geological Survey; 16, U.S. Geological Survey; 18, O.H. Hinsdale Wave Research Laboratory, Oregon State University; 19, Bretwood Higman, University of Washington; 20, NASA; 21 both, Koji Sasahara/ Associated Press; 22, Jose C. Borrero, University of Southern California; 24, Pacific Tsunami Museum; 27, Naval Historical Foundation; 29, Used with permission from the Stars and Stripes. © 1964, 2008 Stars and Stripes; 30, Corbis; 32, NOAA National Data Buoy Center; 33, NOAA West Coast and Alaska Tsunami Warning Center; 34, NOAA National Data Buoy Center; 35, Aaron Favila/ Associated Press; 36, NOAA National Data Buoy Center; 37, David Heikkila/ iStockphoto.com; 38, Tim Laman/ National Geographic Image Collection; 40-41, Adam Powell/ Taxi/ Getty Images; 42, Tatyana Makeyeva/ AFP/ Getty Images; 43, U.S. Geological Survey; 45, Bazuki Muhammad/ Reuters/ Corbis.

On April 2, 2007, a powerful earthquake launched a tsunami
that struck the Solomon Islands in the Pacific Ocean. This
house was pulled a mile offshore as the wave drew back.

CONTENTS

CHAPTER 1

Indian Ocean Tsunami of 2004

"Like Niagara Falls Moving Towards Us"

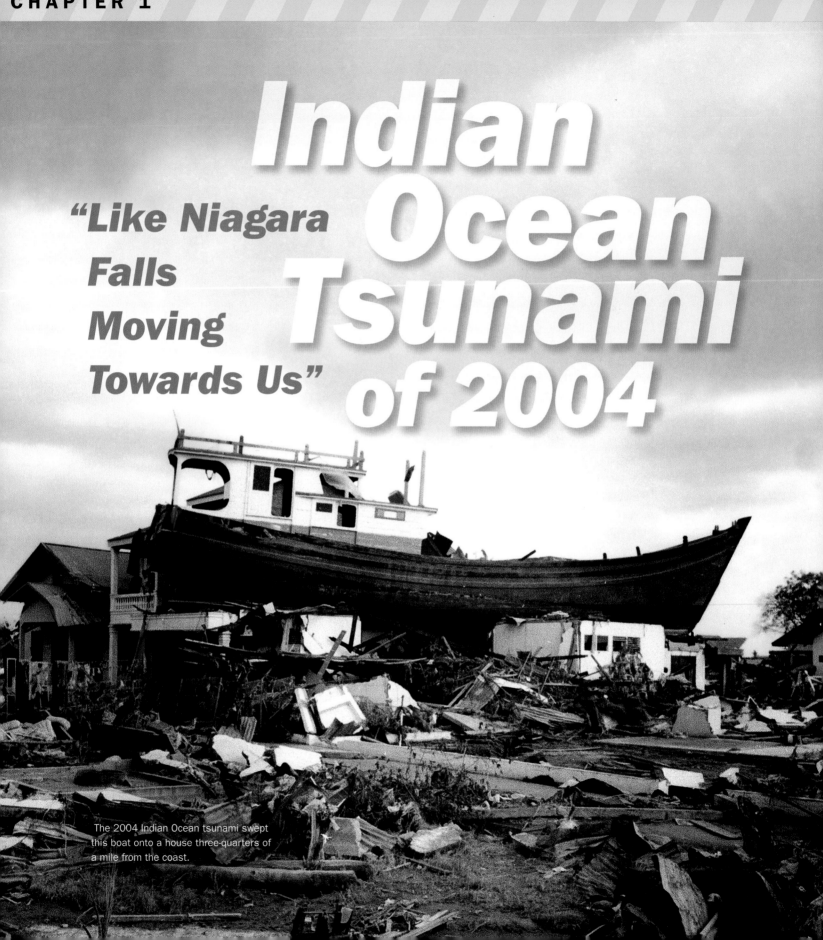

The 2004 Indian Ocean tsunami swept this boat onto a house three-quarters of a mile from the coast.

The Indian Ocean tsunami of 2004 affected millions of people.

On December 26, 2004, an earthquake shook our planet so violently that it wobbled slightly on its axis.

The quake struck shortly after dawn, beneath the floor of the Indian Ocean. Lasting about nine minutes, this was the third most powerful earthquake ever measured. It unleashed a natural disaster of almost unimaginable proportions.

"Chairs, pieces of houses, tables, and trees were floating through the water, which was on both sides of our train as far as the eye could see."

Eranthie Mendis, who survived the 2004 Indian Ocean tsunami aboard a train in Sri Lanka

A large earthquake that occurs beneath or near the ocean can violently disturb seawater, creating a series of waves collectively known as a *tsunami*. Out at sea, tsunami waves move at hundreds of miles per hour but appear as just bumps on the ocean's surface. Approaching shore, they slow down dramatically, but can pile up into titanic walls of water. The December 26, 2004, earthquake triggered tsunami waves that raced toward the shores of more than a dozen countries along the Indian Ocean. Some locales were struck by waves up to 110 feet tall—the height of an 11-story building.

One of the first places hit was Indonesia's Simeulue Island, only 25 miles from the site of the quake. Waves began pounding the island a few minutes after the shaking stopped. Reaching 50 feet in height, the waves destroyed entire villages, yet only seven of the island's 78,000 people died. Warnings handed down by Simeulue islanders for generations accounted for the low death toll.

"Suddenly we saw a huge wave coming... My first impression was, it looked like Niagara Falls moving towards us."

Professor Dipak Jain, recalling his family's close call with a tsunami wave on December 26, 2004, in Phuket, Thailand

Long ago, an earthquake launched a tsunami that devastated Simeulue Island. Ever since, the islanders have taught their young people to run to the hills if they feel an earthquake. When the quake struck in late 2004, islanders shouted *"Semong! Semong!"*—their word for tsunami. By the time the waves arrived, nearly everyone on the island had taken refuge on high ground.

Thirty minutes after the quake, the first in a series of waves struck the Indonesian island of Sumatra. Banda Aceh on Sumatra was the closest major city to the earthquake. Huge waves that sped inland as far as three miles destroyed two-thirds of Banda Aceh and killed tens of thousands of its inhabitants. In all, the tsunami claimed 168,000 lives in Indonesia. On that single day, Indonesia lost more people than have died in all the tornadoes, hurricanes, earthquakes, floods, volcanic eruptions, and tsunamis that have ever struck the United States.

Taken from space, the photo on the left shows the town of Lhoknga on Sumatra's coast before the 2004 tsunami. The photo on the right, taken two days later, shows the destroyed town after the tsunami. One wave may have been as tall as 50 feet when it hit the shore.

As a tsunami wave engulfed nearby boats, Karin Svaerd ran to warn her family. "I could hear people shouting at me 'Get off the beach' as I ran past them—but I ignored them." Karin, her husband, her three sons, and her brother survived the tsunami.

An hour after Indonesia was devastated, waves began to barrage beaches in southern Thailand. On Maikhao Beach in Phuket, Thailand, a ten-year-old schoolgirl from England was vacationing with her parents and seven-year-old sister. Two weeks earlier, in geography class, Tilly Smith had learned about how earthquakes trigger tsunamis. Tilly had been impressed by the fact that, before a tsunami wave strikes, the sea sometimes recedes from the shore.

That Sunday morning, the day after Christmas, Tilly was on the beach with her family when she noticed something odd. "There were bubbles and the tide went out all of a sudden," she later explained. Remembering her geography lessons, Tilly warned her family that a tsunami wave might be coming. As the Smiths left the beach, they told other tourists to also seek higher ground. Thanks to Tilly's warning, by the time the giant waves struck, Maikhao Beach had been evacuated, and no lives were lost there.

On another of Thailand's beaches, several children were reportedly saved when they were placed on an elephant's back and carried to safety before the waves could swallow them. However, tsunami waves drowned 8,000 other people along Thailand's coast.

A half-hour after striking Thailand, waves reached Sri Lanka. As many as six separate waves slammed into this island country. A tragic incident in

This coastal resort in Phuket, Thailand, was engulfed by the Indian Ocean tsunami of December 26, 2004.

Sri Lanka involved a train that ran along the coast. About 1,500 passengers were crowded aboard the *Queen of the Sea* when it was struck by two separate waves. More than 800 passengers drowned, making this one of the deadliest railroad disasters ever. When the waves finished with Sri Lanka, 35,000 people had died.

At about the time the tsunami struck Sri Lanka, waves also hit India, just 20 miles to the north. The waves that rammed India's coast surged as far as two miles inland and killed nearly 20,000 people.

Other Asian countries where waves claimed lives included Myanmar, Malaysia, and the Maldives. The tsunami even reached Africa's eastern coast, killing 300 people in Somalia. The most distant locale where the tsunami took lives was South Africa. There, high water killed several people 16 hours after the earthquake had occurred 5,000 miles to the northeast.

Amidst all the death and destruction were a few amazing survival stories. Malawati Daud,

WITNESS TO A TSUNAMI

"...Then the second wave came—more like a rise of water—and came into our train car. We climbed on the seats but the water rose in seconds. It reached our necks and then I was completely underwater and so was my mother and everyone else in the train car."

Eranthie Mendis, describing her ordeal aboard the *Queen of the Sea* in Sri Lanka

a 23-year-old woman from Sumatra, was swept out to sea with her husband. He soon disappeared beneath the water. Malawati, who couldn't swim and was pregnant, seemed to be doomed. "I was thrashing in the water trying to keep my head up when I chanced upon a tree," Malawati later explained. She survived by holding onto the floating tree, a sago palm, and sustained herself by eating its fruit and bark. After clinging to the tree for five days, she was rescued by a fishing boat.

Ari Afrizal was building a house in the town of Calang, Sumatra, when a wave sucked him out to sea. Ari survived the first day by clutching a log. He then climbed into a damaged wooden boat in which he drifted for a time. After that he built a raft out of passing debris. At first he plucked floating coconuts from the water, but then, he later related, "for three days I didn't eat anything. I gave up all hope of living." On January 9, 2005, Ari was spotted by a ship and rescued. He had spent two full weeks in the ocean and had drifted 200 miles from Calang.

The 2004 disaster left an incredible death toll in its wake. According to the United Nations, 230,000 lives were lost, making the Indian Ocean tsunami by far the deadliest tsunami in recorded history. Hundreds of thousands more suffered injuries, and over a million people lost their homes.

Huge numbers of survivors also lost their means of earning a living as farm fields were flooded, fishing boats were demolished, and shops and hotels were destroyed. It will take decades for the tsunami-ravaged regions to recover—if they ever do.

Two boys search what remains of their home after the Indian Ocean tsunami destroyed it in Banda Aceh, Sumatra.

"A Wave 800 Feet Tall"

Tsunami Science

In 2001, geologist Edward Bryant of Australia published his book *Tsunami: The Underrated Hazard.* The title was appropriate at the time. If anything good emerged from the 2004 Indian Ocean disaster, it is that most people now have a healthy respect for tsunamis.

"You cannot even imagine the power of millions of tons of water in a wave that extends all the way to the ocean's horizon..."

Dr. Dan Walker, tsunami expert

This rare photo was taken from a boat after a tsunami wave passed under the vessel but before it slammed into an island off Thailand during the 2004 disaster.

TSUNAMI "TRIGGERS"

The word *tsunami* is pronounced *sue NAHM ee* or *tsoo NAH mee*. It comes from the Japanese words *tsu*, meaning "harbor," and *nami*, meaning "wave." A tsunami is a series of waves created by disturbances of large bodies of water, usually the ocean.

"All tsunamis are caused by massive displacement of water," explains Cindi Preller, a geologist and tsunami watch specialist based in Palmer, Alaska. "They are triggered events—meaning that various phenomena such as earthquakes, landslides, and volcanoes cause them. Earthquakes are the leading trigger of tsunamis."

Earthquakes occur when underground rock formations snap, causing the ground to shake. If a strong quake takes place beneath or very near the sea, disturbances to the ocean floor can set tsunami waves in motion. In 1964 a huge earthquake near the ocean in Alaska triggered one of the biggest tsunami disasters in United States history. Tsunami waves generated by the 1964 Alaska quake claimed more than 100 lives. Several people died in Crescent City, California, 1,700 miles south of where the earthquake had occurred.

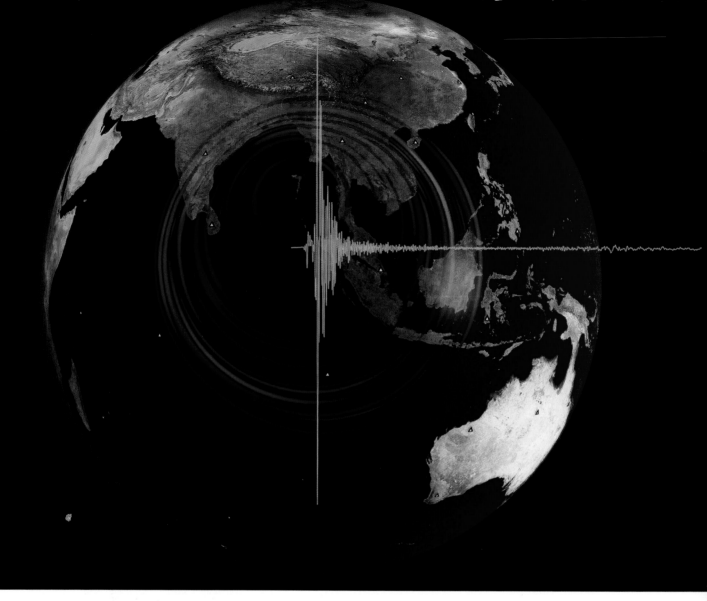

This picture shows the seismographic recording of the underwater earthquake that triggered the 2004 Indian Ocean tsunami. The rings show how far the waves traveled.

Volcanic eruptions on islands and along seacoasts can also disturb the ocean, triggering a tsunami. In 1883, Krakatau Volcano on Indonesia's Krakatau Island produced one of the most stupendous eruptions ever witnessed. The explosion launched tsunami waves that were as tall as a 13-story building.

Undersea landslides are another tsunami trigger. "The ocean floor is not flat," explains Cindi Preller. "It is full of mountains, ridges, and valleys." From time to time, landslides occur beneath the sea. In 1998 an undersea landslide triggered a 30-foot-tall wave and other large tsunami waves that killed 3,000 people in the island nation of Papua New Guinea.

Now and then huge chunks of rock and/or ice from coastal mountains fall into the ocean, generating huge waves. These are called *splash tsunamis* because they result from gigantic ker-plops. One of the largest tsunami waves in history was created this way.

On the night of July 10, 1958, Howard Ulrich and eight-year-old Howard Jr. were sleeping in their fishing boat anchored in Alaska's Lituya Bay. Suddenly they were jostled by an earthquake. "It shook the boat really hard," he recalls. "Even floating on water you could feel it—a

"We got on the roof, which had tar paper shingles we clung to. Then a wave hit—I'd guess it was at least 40 feet high—a huge, dark wall of water coming towards us. The house we were on was ripped off its foundation from the ground level up. We were swirling, spinning, and bouncing like pinballs as we hung onto the shingles."

Doug McRae, of Seward, Alaska, whose family was swirled around in the waters of the 1964 Good Friday tsunami until the house they were on got stuck in some trees.

Dozens of fishing boats were swept into the town of Kodiak, Alaska, by a tsunami in 1964 triggered by the Good Friday Earthquake.

"The splash created a wave that was later estimated at 800 feet tall. It came towards us, taking about four minutes to reach us. It got steadily smaller as it moved along, but it was still about 120 feet high when it hit us. The wave washed our boat over the shoreline. I looked down over the stern [back end] of the boat and saw that we were about 50 feet above the treetops. It felt like an elevator ride. When the wave came back down, it helped bring us away from shore into deep water. Another boat in the bay disappeared in the wave and the couple aboard were never found."

Howard Ulrich, describing how he and his son survived the Lituya Bay megatsunami

Huge trees higher than 1700 feet (518 meters) above Lituya Bay were uprooted by the July 1958 splash tsunami.

long and hard earthquake. It knocked rocks off a mountainside five or six miles from where my son and I were."

An estimated 180 billion (180,000,000,000) pounds of rock and ice tumbled into the water, making a splash that was later determined to be about 1,740 feet high—nearly 500 feet taller than the Empire State Building.

Occasionally comets, asteroids, and large meteorites strike the Earth. Over the past two million years, an estimated 200 to 500 extraterrestrial objects at least several hundred feet in diameter have crashed into our planet. Scientists believe that millions of years ago one such object hit the Earth with such force that the dirt and dust it forced into the atmosphere blocked the sunlight. The blocked sunlight may have contributed to the extinction of many living things, including the dinosaurs.

ANATOMY OF A TSUNAMI

Most tsunamis occur in the Pacific Ocean and along its shores. This is because an area called the Pacific Ring of Fire has 90% of the world's earthquakes and 75% of our planet's volcanoes—two of the leading causes of tsunamis.

EARTHQUAKES AND TSUNAMIS

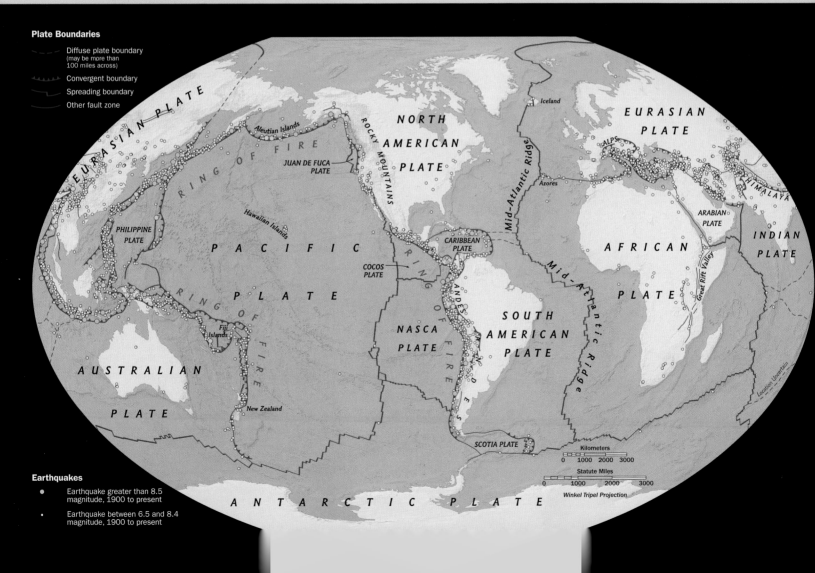

Plate Boundaries

⌐ ⌐ ⌐ Diffuse plate boundary (may be more than 100 miles across)

Convergent boundary

Spreading boundary

Other fault zone

Earthquakes

● Earthquake greater than 8.5 magnitude, 1900 to present

· Earthquake between 6.5 and 8.4 magnitude, 1900 to present

Kilometers
0 1000 2000 3000

Statute Miles
0 1000 2000 3000

Winkel Tripel Projection

However, tsunamis also occur in the Indian Ocean, the Mediterranean Sea, and others of the world's oceans and seas.

"Most every coastline in the world can be affected by tsunamis—either by having a trigger close by or by being struck by a large tsunami formed far afield," explains geologist Alberto M. Lopez-Venegas. "For example, the eastern coast of the U.S. could have a tsunami triggered by submarine landslides offshore. Our eastern coast could also be reached by tsunamis generated in the Caribbean Sea, from Europe, or possibly by volcanic eruptions of islands in the Atlantic Ocean."

The biggest misconception about a tsunami event is that it consists of a single wave. "If you throw a pebble in a pond, will it make only one wave?"

Scientists at Oregon State University create mini-tsunamis in their special wave basin. They then design and test tsunami-resistant model buildings and bridges.

COMPOSITION OF WAVES

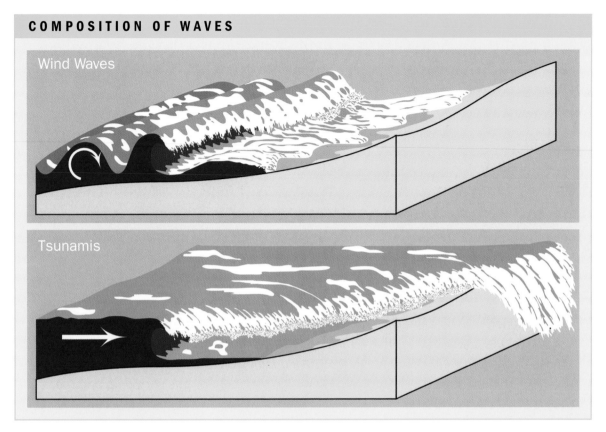

The top drawing shows how regular wind waves ebb and flow normally. The bottom drawing shows how tsunami waves overrun coastlines, sometimes as floods, sometimes as huge walls of water.

asks tsunami expert Preller. "Similarly, a tsunami consists of a series of waves known as a *tsunami wave train*. Rarely are there fewer than ten waves in a tsunami event. Typically there are dozens of waves, large and small. The largest number of waves I ever heard about in a wave train in a given place was 50 or more. Generally the waves occur between 10 and 30 minutes apart, but the time varies depending on the local shoreline. A tsunami wave train can continue for more than 20 hours."

As Tilly Smith knew, the water level sometimes goes down along the seacoast prior to a tsunami wave. This unexpected, rapid withdrawal of the sea is called *drawback*. Dr. Dan Walker, tsunami advisor to the city and county of Honolulu, Hawaii, offers a simplified explanation for this phenomenon: "Waves have valleys as well as peaks. The valleys are what we call drawback."

Drawback is very different from tides—daily rises and falls of the ocean caused by the gravitational attraction of the moon and the sun. "Drawback caused by tsunamis happens very rapidly—over a span of a few minutes," Dr. Walker points out. "Unlike tsunamis, the drawdown of sea level associated with the tides takes several hours."

Scientists refer to a tsunami wave's height as its *amplitude*. Out in the middle of the ocean—where the seabed is a long way down and there is plenty of room for extra water—tsunami waves have an amplitude of less than three feet. "Because tsunami waves in the deep ocean are a few miles long, people on ships far out at sea do not notice the gradual change in sea

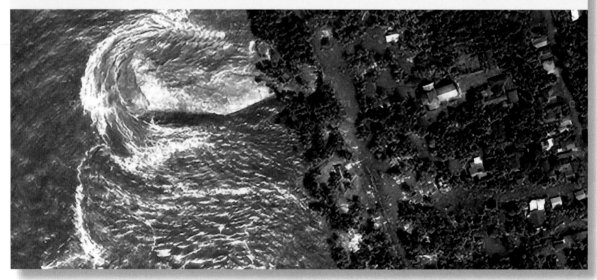

This picture shows the swirl of two tsunami waves—one just reaching the shore and one withdrawing.

As this wave tank experiment in Japan illustrates, the combination of speed and volume makes water a deadly force.

level as those waves pass under their vessels," Dr. Walker explains. As it nears shore—where the seafloor is shallow—a tsunami wave piles up into a wall of water that may be 30 feet high or more. Another misconception is that the first wave in a tsunami wave train is the biggest. Any of the waves in the train may be the highest and most destructive.

When tsunami waves are gigantic—with an amplitude of about 130 feet or more—the event is known as a *megatsunami*. An undersea earthquake in 1737 triggered one of the tallest quake-related waves of recent centuries. This megatsunami, which slammed into the Kamchatka Peninsula in Siberia, Russia, was 210 feet tall—and yet it was only about a quarter the height of Alaska's Lituya Bay megatsunami of 1958.

Tsunamis can also move incredibly fast. Regular ocean waves are driven by the wind and reach maximum speeds of about 50 miles per hour. In the open ocean, tsunami waves attain roughly ten times that velocity.

The 2004 Indian Ocean tsunami stripped this Indonesian island of vegetation to a height of more than 65 feet.

Maximum speeds for tsunamis are about 700 miles per hour—"comparable to the speed of a jet fighter," says Cindi Preller.

When they pile up into mountains of water and come ashore, tsunami waves slow down to about 40 miles per hour due to friction with the Earth's surface. The fastest the world's fastest humans can run for a short distance is about 25 miles per hour. This means that people cannot get away from a tsunami wave once it is bearing down on them. The only way to escape it is to flee before it arrives.

HOW TSUNAMIS KILL AND DESTROY

Even as recently as late 2004, few people knew much about tsunamis, and even fewer knew their warning signs. This lack of knowledge about tsunamis was a big reason why the Indian Ocean tsunami claimed such a huge death toll. For example, as the drawback of the ocean occurred in a number of places following the quake, thousands of sightseers walked out to explore and even photograph the exposed ocean bottom. For many, it was the last thing they did, as the waves soon arrived and swept them to their death.

Tsunami waves actually have two chances to drown people. The first is when they smash their way inland. The second is when they retreat back toward the sea. Both Malawati Daud and Ari Afrizal survived tsunami waves, only to be swept out into the Indian Ocean and nearly drowned when the floodwaters retreated.

But tsunamis don't just take lives by drowning their victims. Each cubic foot of seawater weighs 64 pounds, and there are millions of cubic feet of seawater in a tsunami wave. The moving water—and the tree limbs, automobiles, rocks, and parts of houses in it—can batter people to death.

An example of the tremendous power of water occurred during the 1983 Sea of Japan tsunami. The water picked up a concrete block weighing more than *two million* pounds and moved it 500 feet across a beach over 20-foot-tall sand dunes.

"When you are running from an eight-foot wall of water, you have no doubt about the power of the ocean!"

Jeanne Branch Johnston, survivor of the 1946 tsunami in Hawaii.

Although water is used to put them out, fires are another tsunami hazard. The waves split open gasoline storage tanks and other containers filled with flammable liquids and gases. These substances catch fire or explode when the tanks collide or when sparks or electric wires touch them. Seward, Alaska's waterfront caught fire when the 1964 quake caused oil tanks to explode and oil-slicked tsunami waters spread the flames.

In the next chapter, we will see how some famous tsunamis have caused death and destruction.

CHAPTER 3

Some Historic Tsunamis

"Everything Had Become Sea"

A 1946 earthquake near Alaska's Aleutian Islands spawned a tsunami that destroyed buildings in Hilo, Hawaii, more than 2,300 miles away. In this rare photograph, the wave can be seen in the distance as the photographer takes one last picture before running for safety.

> **"We were awakened by a loud hissing sound, as if dozens of locomotives were blowing off steam outside our house. We jumped up and rushed to the front window. Where there had been a beach, we saw nothing but water, which was coming directly at the house."**
>
> Geologist **Francis Shepard,** describing Hawaii's April Fools' Day tsunami of 1946

Tsunamis that occurred before written records are called *paleotsunamis*, meaning "ancient tsunamis." Geologists learn about paleotsunamis, such as the paleo-megatsunami that seems to have contributed to the dinosaurs' extinction, by uncovering evidence of ancient sea floods. More, however, is known about tsunamis of recent centuries.

TWO JAPANESE TSUNAMIS: 1771 AND 1792

Over the past 13 centuries, Japan has suffered about 200 tsunami disasters—more than any other country during that period. Japan's earliest recorded tsunami struck in 684 A.D. Two of its most devastating tsunamis occurred more than a thousand years later in the 18th century.

In April 1771, a powerful undersea earthquake shook the vicinity of Okinawa Island, which today is part of Japan. Despite the quake's intensity, not a single death was reported as a direct result of the trembling of the ground. However, the quake generated tsunami waves that, according to old reports, exceeded 100 feet in height. The titanic waves killed 12,000 people on several Japanese islands. This tsunami also caused crop failures and outbreaks of disease that killed thousands more.

Twenty years later in late 1791, earthquakes began to shake Unzen Volcano on the island of Kyushu, Japan. Early the next year, the volcano erupted,

> *"We ran as fast as we could and went through someone's backyard to get as far from the ocean as we could. We finally stopped somewhere near the radio tower. I climbed up a tree and saw a huge wave wash over a telephone pole. In the afternoon we made our way back to the road and the sight was of unbelievable destruction— demolished houses, uprooted trees, twisted furniture, large boulders, and bodies."*

Jeanne Branch Johnston, recalling how she survived the April Fools' Day tsunami in Hawaii at the age of 6

belching out lava. On May 21, 1792, part of Unzen Volcano collapsed due to the volcanic eruptions, the continuing earthquakes, or a combination of the two. The volcano's collapse triggered a landslide that traveled four miles before tumbling into the sea, where it generated gigantic tsunami waves. An estimated 15,000 people died in this disaster, two-thirds of them in the waves and the rest in the landslide.

"THIS MONSTROUS WAVE": THE 1868 TSUNAMI IN PERU AND CHILE

On August 13, 1868, a powerful earthquake rocked the Pacific Ocean seabed near what is now the border between Chile and Peru in South America. The quake severely damaged Arica, a city which then belonged to Peru but today is part of Chile.

Within a half-hour of the quake, a tsunami wave train began battering coastal communities in Chile and Peru. The second wave was the monster. It rose 90 feet high when it hit the shore. In Arica, the combination of earthquake and waves killed about 25,000 people.

The waves also picked up ships in Arica's harbor. The *Fredonia*, a U.S. Navy ship, was dashed to pieces against a cliff, killing all but two of 29 crew members aboard.

The earthquake and waves killed up to 70,000 people along the coasts of Peru and Chile, making this one of South America's worst natural disasters ever. Tsunami waves also caused extensive damage at great distances. They battered Hawaii, 6,000 miles from the site of the quake, and even slammed into New Zealand, some 8,000 miles from Arica.

It had been dark for some time when the lookout said that a wave was coming. Staring into the night, we first made out a thin phosphorescent line, which seemed to be rising higher and higher. The wave that we had dreaded for hours was upon us.

We could do nothing but watch this monstrous wave approach. With a terrifying din, our ship was buried under a half-liquid, half-solid mass of sand and water. We stayed under for a suffocating eternity. Then, groaning, our Wateree pushed her way to the surface, with her gasping crew still hanging on to the rails.

We were high and dry, two miles inland. The wave had carried us at an unbelievable speed over the sand dunes which line the shore, across a valley, and beyond the railway line. If the wave had carried us another 60 yards, it would have smashed us against the mountain wall.

The U.S. Navy ship *Wateree* was also in Arica's harbor that fateful day in 1868. **Lieutenant L. G. Billings** recorded his experience.

The *Wateree* after the tsunami.

"I TURNED AND RAN FOR MY LIFE": KRAKATAU, 1883

On August 27, 1883, Indonesia's Krakatau Volcano exploded in one of the mightiest eruptions of all time. This eruption, which was heard up to 3,000 miles away, shot an ash cloud 50 miles into the sky. Fortunately no one lived on Krakatau Island, most of which was destroyed, but the volcano had another way to kill.

The eruption sent tsunami waves racing toward the Indonesian islands of Java and Sumatra at 300 miles per hour. The waves were as much as 130 feet tall. They were so powerful that they picked up masses of coral weighing up to 12 million pounds and carried them ashore.

At that time, much of Indonesia was ruled by the Dutch. A Dutch ship pilot later described what happened when the giant waves struck Anjer Lor, a town on Java:

> *At first it seemed like a low range of hills rising out of the water. A second glance convinced me that it was a ridge of water many feet high. I turned and ran for my life. In a few minutes I heard the water with a loud roar break upon the shore. I was taken off my feet and borne inland.*
>
> *The waters swept past, and I found myself clinging to a coconut palm tree. Most of the trees near the town were uprooted and thrown down for miles, but this one fortunately had escaped and myself with it.*
>
> *The huge wave rolled on, gradually decreasing in height and strength until the mountain slopes at the back of Anjer were reached, and then, its fury spent, the waters gradually receded and flowed back into the sea. As I clung to the palm tree, wet and exhausted, there floated past the dead bodies of many a friend and neighbor. Only a handful of the population escaped, and scarcely a trace remains of the once busy, thriving town where my life has been spent.*

The Krakatau tsunami destroyed some 200 towns and villages on Java and Sumatra and killed approximately 36,000 people. This was one of the world's deadliest tsunamis prior to the Indian Ocean catastrophe of 2004.

"WE STARTED RUNNING": ALASKA AND HAWAII, 1946

The Hawaiian Islands, located in the middle of the Pacific Ocean, have often been hit by tsunamis. So have Alaska and its Aleutian Islands, which are very active segments of the Pacific Ring of Fire. One of the United States' worst tsunami disasters occurred in 1946, when Alaska and Hawaii were U.S. territories but had not yet achieved statehood.

In the early hours of April 1, a big earthquake shook the ocean bottom about 100 miles from Alaska's Unimak Island in the Aleutians. The quake launched a tsunami wave train. Minutes after the quake, a 100-foot-high wall of water slammed into Unimak Island. The gigantic wave pulverized Scotch Cap Lighthouse on the island, killing its five-man Coast Guard crew.

Waves created by the Alaskan quake sped across the Pacific Ocean at 500 miles per hour. The first one took four and a half hours to travel some 2,300 miles to the Hawaiian Islands. Walls of water up to 55 feet high battered the islands, sweeping away homes, hotels, roads, bridges, railroad tracks, and automobiles.

As the mountains of water approached, people rushed about to warn their neighbors, many of whom fled to high ground.

Unfortunately, though, some people thought the warnings were an April Fools' prank and refused to leave. To this day, the April 1, 1946 disaster is called the April Fools' Day tsunami in Hawaii.

18 years after the 1946 April Fools' Day tsunami, Alaska was the site of another powerful quake, which generated the 1964 Good Friday tsunami. This page from *Stars and Stripes*, the United States Armed Forces newspaper, describes the destruction caused by that tsunami.

One hard-hit region was the northern side of Hawaii's Oahu Island. Marine geologist Francis Shepard, who lived in this area, later described how he and his wife barely escaped the waves:

We started running along the beach ridge to the slightly elevated main road. As we ran, another huge wave came rolling in over the reef. Rising as a monstrous wall of water, it swept on after us, flattening [a] cane field with a terrifying sound. We reached the comparative safety of the elevated road just ahead of the wave.

The April Fools' Day tsunami destroyed these buildings in Hilo, Hawaii.

Finally, after about 6 waves had moved in, each one getting weaker, I decided I had better go back and see what I could rescue from what was left of the house. I had just reached the door when I became conscious that a very powerful mass of water was bearing down on the place. I rushed to a nearby tree and climbed it as fast as possible and then hung on for dear life as I swayed back and forth under the impact of the wave. The wave soon subsided, and the series of waves that followed were all minor in comparison.

The tsunami killed at least 159 people in the Hawaiian Islands. The city of Hilo on the "Big Island" of Hawaii suffered the most. There, waves claimed 96 lives and destroyed nearly all of the waterfront business district.

Besides Alaska and Hawaii, waves struck the coast of Chile and coastal areas of Washington, Oregon, and California. One person drowned at Santa Cruz, California, raising the death toll of the April Fools' Day tsunami to at least 165.

"MY ARMS WERE EMPTY": PHILIPPINES TSUNAMI OF 1976

The Philippines, an island nation in the Pacific Ocean, has been another frequent site of earthquakes and tsunamis. Shortly after midnight on August 17, 1976, a powerful quake shook the seabed near Mindanao, second largest of the more than 7,000 Philippine islands. The undersea quake launched tsunami waves toward Mindanao and several other islands of the Philippines.

The highest wave was 15 feet—not extremely tall for a tsunami. But what they lacked in size, the waves more than made up for in suddenness. The first wave smashed into coastal regions of the Philippines just five minutes after the quake. Because they came unexpectedly and struck in the middle of the night, the waves caught thousands of coastal residents totally by surprise. Waves extensively damaged cities on Mindanao Island, destroyed a dozen fishing villages, and took thousands of lives.

By the time the water subsided, about 8,000 lives had been lost. Nine-tenths of the victims were carried off by the waves, while the rest died in the earthquake. A hundred thousand people were left homeless in one of the deadliest earthquake and tsunami disasters ever to strike the Philippines.

> *"Everybody was crying and shouting and warning of a wave coming at us. I tried to gather all my five children into my arms. When the waves swept us out with our house, I found that my arms were empty. I wanted to shout and curse my misery, but I had no more voice. It was then that I saw my little girl, her small fingers disappearing into the water, waving for help that never came."*

Gloria Bitancor, describing her tragic experience to *Time* magazine

CHAPTER 4

"Out of the Blue"

Tsunami Warnings and Safety

Crew members of the NOAA research ship *Ronald H. Brown* position a DART buoy in the Pacific Ocean.

Tsunami experts have a saying: "If you can see the tsunami, it is too late." In recent decades, scientists have improved their ability to detect tsunamis and warn people *before* they strike.

Scientists at the West Coast and Alaska Tsunami Warning Center issue worldwide watches and warnings when tsunami-generating earthquakes occur.

TSUNAMI WARNING SYSTEMS

After the 1946 April Fools' Day catastrophe, the United States established a tsunami warning system for Hawaii. Its headquarters near Honolulu, Hawaii, is called the Pacific Tsunami Warning Center. Following Alaska's 1964 disaster,

"We monitor the planet's pulse..."

Cindi Preller, tsunami scientist

the U.S. established a warning system for Alaska, too. Its headquarters at Palmer, Alaska, is called the West Coast and Alaska Tsunami Warning Center. Over the years, the two centers' areas of responsibility have expanded greatly. Between them, these two facilities warn of possible tsunamis in Hawaii, Alaska, and other U.S. and Canadian coastal regions, plus locales around the Pacific Ocean, Indian Ocean, and Caribbean Sea.

Several other tsunami warning systems now exist. The International Pacific Tsunami Warning System, based at the Pacific Tsunami Warning Center in Hawaii, provides information about possible tsunamis for 20-plus countries in or along the Pacific Ocean including Australia, Canada, Chile, China, Guatemala, Indonesia, Japan, Mexico, the Philippines, and the United

States. The nation that has been hit the most by tsunamis has its own system, the Japanese Tsunami Warning Service. French Polynesia, a group of some 120 Pacific islands, also has a tsunami warning system, as does Chile.

The warning centers receive information from a network of seismometers stationed around the world. Seismometers are instruments that detect and measure earthquakes. When seismometers reveal that a large earthquake has occurred beneath or near the ocean, the warning centers know that a tsunami might soon take aim on coastal regions.

But the warning centers need more information prior to issuing bulletins to local authorities who make decisions about evacuating seacoasts. Did the earthquake actually generate a tsunami? Where are the waves headed? And what about tsunamis caused by volcanoes, under–sea landslides, and other phenomena? Scientists have developed ways to gather such data.

As they cross the ocean, tsunamis alter the level of the sea slightly. Tsunami warning centers rely on instruments placed in the oceans to monitor the sea's height. For example, the U.S. tsunami program includes *Tsunameters* that sit on the seafloor. As a tsunami passes, the water pressure rises due to an increase in the

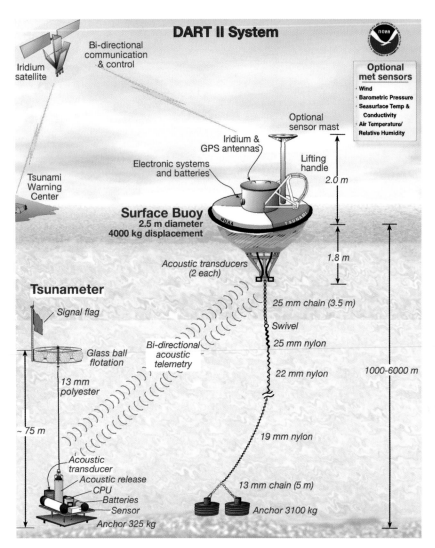

DART stands for Deep-ocean Assessment and Reporting of tsunamis. It is the tsunami warning system operated by the United States. DART allows for real-time tsunami detection as waves travel across open waters.

amount of water. Deep-sea pressure detectors measure these tsunami-created pressure increases. They transmit their data to buoys on the ocean surface. These floating instruments relay the information to satellites orbiting Earth, which then send the data to tsunami warning centers. The warning centers also receive information from tide gauges—instruments located on islands and mainland coasts that monitor changes in sea level.

Tsunami warning centers issue bulletins similar to those given for tornadoes and hurricanes. A *tsunami watch* means that there is a possibility of a tsunami and that people should be alert for further instructions. A *tsunami warning* means that an actual tsunami is a strong possibility and may strike certain locales, which should be evacuated immediately. The bulletins are sent from tsunami warning centers by fax, e-mail, telephone, and other means to public officials who make the final decision about whether an evacuation is necessary. The public is then informed over commercial radio and TV about the tsunami alert and advised on what actions to take. Some

In May 2006 villagers in the Philippenes evacuate their homes next to a sign that reads "TSUNAMI—THIS WAY TO A SAFE PLACE." The Philippines joined two dozen other nations in an ocean-wide evacuation drill testing the tsunami warning systems and people's responses to them.

coastal communities alert people to flee by setting off sirens or by using public address systems. For example, communities in Hawaii, Oregon, and Thailand sound sirens when tsunamis are expected, and some cities even hold "tsunami drills" so people will be prepared should a real tsunami strike.

Tsunami warning systems have saved lives in Hawaii, Japan, and other locales. There has also been a colossal failure. There were no warnings for most places prior to the killer Indian Ocean tsunami of late 2004. The reason was that, unlike the Pacific Ocean, the Indian Ocean had no tsunami warning system. Had such a system been in place, tens of thousands of lives might have been saved. Soon after that disaster, all 27 countries bordering the Indian Ocean began setting up a tsunami warning network for the region under the United Nations' direction. Known as the Indian Ocean Tsunami

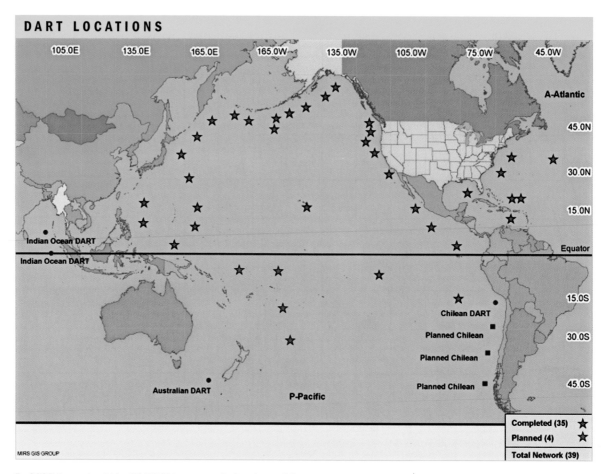

By 2009 there should be 39 DART buoys monitoring the world's oceans.

Warning and Mitigation System, it began operating in mid-2006 with the Pacific Tsunami Warning Center in Hawaii as its interim headquarters. However, as of 2008 many improvements were still needed before the system could work properly.

ANIMAL INSTINCT—NATURE'S WARNING

Animals may sense impending natural disasters before humans are aware of them. Eyewitnesses reported many instances of animals behaving strangely in the hours and minutes before the tsunami waves struck in 2004.

Well before a wave hit, visitors to a national park in Sri Lanka saw three elephants running toward higher ground. At a wildlife sanctuary in India, flamingos unexpectedly flew to higher ground before a wave roared in. Dogs refused to go outside for their daily walks along coastal beaches, their owners later reported. Zoo animals and bats also behaved oddly before the waves struck.

Their superior senses of hearing, smell, and touch may have alerted animals to the fact that something unusual was about to occur. Elephants, for example, have sensitive bones in their feet that may have enabled them to feel vibrations caused by onrushing waves. And, as every dog owner knows, their pets have much better hearing than humans do.

"It is wise to trust animal behavior in any natural disaster," advises tsunami scientist Cindi Preller. "If my dog was looking at the ocean in fear, or started to run away from the ocean as fast as she could, I'd follow her and trust her instincts."

LEARNING FROM OUR MISTAKES

Some countries have methods to mitigate tsunamis, or make them less disastrous. In Japan

An Asian elephant

Mangroves are often found in coastal areas. The unique roots of mangrove trees help trap and hold sediment washed in with the tides.

and Hawaii, sea walls have been constructed along tsunami-prone coasts. These walls can't completely block a large tsunami. However, they can slow the waves and reduce their wallop. Japan has also built tsunami shelters along certain beaches. People who can't flee the seacoast in time can seek safety in these shelters.

Natural barriers such as trees, sand dunes, and coral reefs also mitigate tsunamis by partially blocking the giant waves. For example, the 2004 tsunami claimed few lives in certain villages in India and Sri Lanka because forests near shore absorbed much of the waves' impact. Unfortunately, though, human beings have destroyed coastal forests, sand dunes, and coral reefs in many places, leaving these locales especially vulnerable to tsunami waves. Since 2004 there has been a movement in Indian Ocean countries and elsewhere to conserve the barriers that nature has provided against tsunamis.

Trees such as mangroves and coconut palms are also being planted in coastal regions where tsunamis may strike. Besides slowing the waves, the trees can be held onto or climbed by people who have no other way to escape.

WHAT CAN YOU DO?

The saying "expect the unexpected" is fitting for tsunamis. Some tsunamis travel thousands of miles and do immense damage. Others strike nearby shores yet do little harm. The sea recedes before some tsunamis strike. With others, the first sign of the tsunami is the giant wave itself. The first wave is the most dangerous in some tsunami events. With others, a later wave is the big killer. The best protection against all the unexpected dangers of tsunamis is to follow some safety tips.

Coastal residents should have a tsunami evacuation plan. Know where nearby high ground is and figure out the best route to get there. If there is no high ground nearby, plan the quickest way to get at least a mile inland—preferably on foot because automobiles may get stuck in traffic on low-lying roads. The moment you hear a tsunami warning for your area, flee to your place of safety. Never assume that the danger is over after one or two waves. Wait until there have been no waves for many hours, or until emergency officials give the "all-clear" signal, before returning to a coastal residence. It is better to wait too long than not long enough.

Some tsunamis appear so quickly and suddenly that alerts can't be issued in time. To survive such events, people must save themselves. "If you feel or suspect an earthquake and are in a low-lying coastal area, do not wait for a warning," advises Dan Walker. "A tsunami may soon strike, so go quickly to higher ground or further inland." Of course, the same is true if you witness a sudden drawback of the ocean, Walker adds.

The ocean exhibits other oddities prior to some tsunamis. The water may start bubbling strangely or turn unusually hot. Witnesses have heard the ocean make whistling sounds or noises similar to jet airplanes or speeding trains before a tsunami arrives. If you experience any of these things, don't take a chance. Head away from the ocean.

Don't let the remote possibility of a tsunami spoil your fun at the seaside. Yet the great waves do appear from time to time, so it is smart to know their warning signs and what to do if one approaches. As was the case for ten-year-old Tilly Smith and her family, understanding tsunamis can be a lifesaver.

In wilderness is the preservation of the world.

Henry David Thoreau

Coral reefs are nature's way of
reducing the destructive force
of a tsunami.

Glossary

amplitude—a tsunami's height

asteroids—rocky objects, sometimes large, that are located mainly in space between Mars and Jupiter

buoys—floating devices on a body of water's surface; they are often used for guiding ships and in some cases for scientific purposes

comets—space objects made of ice, dust, metal, gases, and rock that have long glowing tails when near the sun

coral—limestone formations created in the ocean by zillions of tiny animals

deep-sea pressure detectors—instruments that sit on the seafloor and detect tsunamis by measuring increases in water pressure

drawback—the unexpected, rapid withdrawal of the sea that sometimes occurs before a tsunami wave

Dutch—the people of the Netherlands

earthquake—the shaking of the ground caused by the breaking of underground rocks

evacuate—to leave an area for safety reasons

geologists—scientists who study rocks, mountains, and other aspects of the Earth

Advancing and retreating tsunami waves pushed and pulled this railroad track out of line.

landslides—the fast-moving slide of rocks, dirt, and other material down slopes (including underwater slopes)

megatsunamis—tsunamis with waves about 130 feet high or more

meteorites—stone and/or metal objects from space that strike our planet

mitigate—to make something less harmful

Pacific Ring of Fire—a ring-shaped chain of volcanoes and earthquake regions encircling the Pacific Ocean

paleotsunamis—tsunamis that occurred before there were written records

seismometers—instruments that detect and measure earthquakes

splash tsunamis—tsunamis that are a result of huge chunks of rocks and/or ice falling into the ocean from coastal mountains

tide gauges—instruments located on islands and mainland coasts that monitor changes in sea level

tsunamis—series of water waves produced by earthquakes, volcanoes, and other disturbances that occur beneath or near the sea

tsunami warning—a bulletin stating that an actual tsunami is a strong possibility and may strike certain locales which should be evacuated immediately

tsunami watch—a bulletin stating that a tsunami is possible and that people should be alert for further instructions

tsunami wave train—a series of tsunami waves

volcanoes—the openings in the ground through which hot rock erupts; the mountains the eruptions create are also called volcanoes

The power of the 1964 Alaska tsunami forced a wooden plank through this super-strong truck tire in Whittier, Alaska.

Further Reading and Research

FOR FURTHER READING

Fine, Jil. *Tsunamis*. New York: Children's Press, 2007.

Hamilton, John. *Tsunamis*. Edina, Minnesota: Abdo Publishing, 2006.

Karwoski, Gail Langer. *Tsunami: The True Story of an April Fools' Day Disaster*. Plain City, Ohio: Darby Creek Publishing, 2006.

Malaspina, Ann. *Tsunamis*. New York: Rosen Publishing, 2007.

Morris, Ann, and Heidi Larson. *Tsunami: Helping Each Other*. Minneapolis, Minnesota: Millbrook Press, 2005.

Stewart, Gail B. *Catastrophe in Southern Asia: The Tsunami of 2004*. Detroit: Lucent Books, 2005.

SOME WEBSITES TO EXPLORE

Basic facts about tsunamis from National Geographic Kids:
http://www.nationalgeographic.com/ngkids/9610/kwave/index.html

Frequently asked questions, with answers and pictures, relating to tsunamis:
http://www.drgeorgepc.com/TsunamiFAQ.html

National Oceanic and Atmospheric Administration (NOAA) tsunami Website containing lots of information:
http://www.tsunami.noaa.gov/

Summary of what happened in the countries hit by the 2004 Indian Ocean tsunami:
http://news.bbc.co.uk/2/hi/asia-pacific/4126019.stm

Information about weird animal behavior prior to the Indian Ocean tsunami:
http://news.nationalgeographic.com/news/2005/01/0104_050104_tsunami_animals.html

Bibliography

Bryant, Edward. *Tsunami: The Underrated Hazard*. Cambridge, England: Cambridge University Press, 2001.

Dudley, Walter C., and Min Lee. *Tsunami!* Honolulu: University of Hawaii Press, 1988.

Krauss, Erich. *Wave of Destruction*. Emmaus, Pennsylvania: Rodale, 2006.

Murty, T. S. *Seismic Sea Waves: Tsunamis*. Ottawa, Canada: Department of Fisheries and the Environment, Fisheries and Marine Service, 1977.

Myles, Douglas. *The Great Waves*. New York: McGraw-Hill, 1985.

Powers, Dennis M. *The Raging Sea*. New York: Citadel Press, 2005.

Prager, Ellen J. *Furious Earth: The Science and Nature of Earthquakes, Volcanoes, and Tsunamis*. New York: McGraw-Hill, 2000.

In Thailand, hundreds of people gather at a memorial service in rememberance of lives lost to the 2004 tsunami.

Interviews by the Authors

SCIENTISTS

Delores Clark, NOAA Public Affairs Officer, Honolulu, Hawaii

Dr. Bruce Jaffe, geologist/oceanographer, United States Geological Survey, Santa Cruz, California

Jeanne Branch Johnston, Earthquake and Tsunami Program Manager, State of Hawaii, Civil Defense Division

William Knight, oceanographer, West Coast and Alaska Tsunami Warning Center, Palmer, Alaska

Dr. Alberto M. Lopez-Venegas, Woods Hole Science Center, Eastern Region, United States Geological Survey

Cindi Preller, geologist and tsunami watch specialist, West Coast and Alaska Tsunami Warning Center, Palmer, Alaska

Brian Shiro, geophysicist, Pacific Tsunami Warning Center, Honolulu, Hawaii

Dr. Dan Walker, tsunami advisor to the City and County of Honolulu, Hawaii

EYEWITNESSES TO TSUNAMIS

Bruce Jaffe (Indonesia)

Dipak Jain (Thailand)

Jeanne Branch Johnston (Hawaii)

Doug McRae (Alaska)

Eranthie Mendis (Sri Lanka)

Howard Ulrich (Alaska)

Dan Walker (Hawaii)

Acknowledgments

ABOUT OUR EXPERTS

Cindi Preller, geologist and tsunami watch specialist, West Coast and Alaska Tsunami Warning Center, Palmer, Alaska

"I am from Colorado and became interested in rocks as soon as I noticed their beauty and how different they are from each other. At about eight years old, I was haunted by the mountains and their different patterns. However, geology wasn't my passion until I discovered it in college by accident as an elective. I had thought I wanted to be a chemist.

"The Indian Ocean tsunami shocked me as well as the rest of the world. A friend of mine works here, and I was immediately interested when a job opened up. We monitor the planet's pulse, recording every earthquake as the Earth recycles and shifts. If a quake is big enough in a region known to be a rascal, then we'll issue a tsunami warning. When tsunamis and earthquakes aren't happening, we develop software to make our analysis more accurate and faster. We also answer questions from everyone, be it a third grader doing a science fair project, a worried relative, or a high-profile news reporter. Every call is equal.

"My daughter, Willow, the coolest human on the planet, just turned 12. Our family includes the two of us, a couple of crazy happy dogs, and a load of fish. We love to travel, swim, dance, hike, kayak, play games, read, and relax together. I collect sand and am extremely fond of music, ravens, and milk chocolate."

Dr. Dan Walker, tsunami advisor to the City and County of Honolulu, Hawaii

"I grew up having 'Tom Sawyer' summers along the Vermilion River at my grandfather's boatyard on the shores of Lake Erie. In a few years my adventures expanded to islands throughout the Pacific, first as a graduate student and eventually as a seismologist [someone who studies earthquakes and their effects like tsunamis] at the University of Hawaii.

"To all you young readers out there, know that science can be a great adventure, that making discoveries about our world is a wonderful experience in itself, and that if you become a scientist, your discoveries could help to improve the quality of life for future generations.

"I'm married with three sons, one daughter, and three grandchildren. I make and install tsunami instruments in Hawaii. I write research articles and educational materials on tsunamis, and stories about my adventures in the Pacific. I ride a bike, run, and swim in my ocean. I try to stay young and do triathlons. Aloha!"

If you have a question about tsunamis, or if you want to talk about tsunamis, feel free to contact the authors. Dennis and Judy can be reached at fradinbooks@comcast.net

Index